What Do I Do Now?

When No New Direction Is Direction

Jim Rogahn

Scripture taken from the New King James Version. Copyright © 1982 by Thomas Nelson, Inc. Used by permission. All rights reserved.

Copyright © 2020 Jim Rogahn

www.jimrogahn.org

All rights reserved

ISBN: 9798684899133

This book and others by Jim Rogahn are available on Amazon around the world.

Table Of Contents

1. What Do I Do Now? 7

2. What Does God's Word Say? 27

3. What Has The Holy Spirit Said? 45

4. What Opportunities Do You Have? 65

5. What Should I Do Now? 81

Preface

Every sincere Christian wants to find and fulfill the will of God. The question is, how do we do that? How do we find out what the will of God is, and then how do we make that a reality in our life?

Another similar question that people have is, how do we go from where we are now to where we want to be? How do we move from the situations we are currently in to the place where we have the need met, and the questions answered?

Not knowing the answers to these questions, or knowing where to find these answers, can be very frustrating. I have talked to people who did not know what to do. They not only had a sense of frustration, but they also felt stagnated in their calling and relationship with God.

God is not withholding or hiding His will from us, that is not the case at all. But, the question remains, how do we find and fulfill the will of God? The goal of this book is to help to give that answer.

1. What Do I Do Now?

It was back in the mid-1980s that I first realized that God had a plan for my life that included going to a Bible school. It was something I knew God wanted me to do, but exactly how it was going to happen was a mystery to me.

Fortunately, I did get to Rhema Bible Training College and I did graduate. But the process it took for me to get there was a big step in my learning how to follow God's direction in my life.

There have been several times like this that I had no idea what to do next, and that is not a nice place to be. When I was in Bible school, I remember wondering what I would do after graduation. And then, when I knew God was leading me to move to Europe, I had no clue how to do it.

In each of these situations, I had some direction from God, but exactly how I was going to do what I needed to do was the issue. In my experience this is a fairly typical situation for many people.

My question was the same question that other people have, what do I do now? And beyond that, it is one thing to know what to do, but then we need to know how to do it.

Some people believe that God gives us a basic plan about what to do, and then we have to figure things out on our own, I am glad that this is not the case. Some people think that God is only interested in the "big things" or "big problems" in our life. The idea is that all of the little, not so important things, He just leaves up to us.

God wants to help us with every, and any, problem we may have, not just the "big" problems that we face. This is why we need to learn how God leads us, and then follow the direction and wisdom that He gives to us.

While it is certainly true that we can pick out our own socks to wear, God is interested in everything that happens in our life and He can help us with all of it. Thank God He did give us a brain to use, and there are many simple things we are involved in every day that we can just take care of on our own, like picking out our own socks.

But we also don't want to neglect the wisdom of God if it is available to us, do we? If God is truly our loving heavenly Father and He wants to help us, shouldn't we also want to learn how He will do that, and how that will happen in our life?

No New Direction Is Direction

One aspect of following God's direction is something I have just learned recently, even though as I look back, this principle is something I have seen happen in my life in the past.

What I have learned is that there are times that no new direction is direction. This is something that I did not understand for many years, and I believe that many people do not really understand it now; this is part of why I have written this book.

We sometimes view God's plan for our life as a continual progression in a certain direction, moving forward in the sense of going from one thing to the next. But, our view of things and our methods are often not the same as God's view and methods.

Rather than see things in a sort of straight line, moving ahead sense, I believe it is better to look at God's plan for our life as a progression from one level to another. By that I mean that while we may move forward, we may also not "move" at all, but we can still learn and develop in a specific thing right where we are.

For example, you can go outside and run as a way to get some exercise. While you are running, you are developing your body and you are also moving from one place to another. But you could also use a treadmill to run on, and even though you are not moving forward or going anywhere different, you are still developing your body.

Both of these examples are working towards the same result, even though they are two different methods. To say that you are only really running while you are running outside is not true. By either running outside or on a treadmill you are still running and exercising your body.

This is similar to God's direction in our life. There are times we will be following God's direction and we see changes taking place and things happening. But there can be other times that God is working in our life and He is developing something in us where we don't notice anything happening.

The idea of no new direction is direction is that there will be times in our life that God has given us direction in some way and we simply need to keep following that direction. We might think it is time for something to change, but God is working in a way we do not see.

We could spend a lot of time looking around for the next thing to do when God has already told us what to do. This is where people tend to get frustrated because they don't understand that God is working in their life, but not in a visible way.

No new direction is direction means that we don't have to constantly ask God, "What do I do now?", but instead we continue doing what God has told us to do until He tells us something else. This book explains that idea.

So, how do we go from where we are now to where we need to be? How can we make the plan, dream, or vision that we have from God come true?

God Has A Plan

As with anything, you have to start with the basics. We first need to realize that God does have a plan for our life. Then we need to learn how to find God's plan and fulfill it.

Ephesians 5:17 (NKJV)
17 Therefore do not be unwise, but understand what the will of the Lord is.

The Bible tells us plainly that we need to understand the will of the Lord. For us to understand God's will, His plan, this has to mean that God does have a plan; God is not just making things up day by day.

God has a plan and He wants to see that plan come to pass. And, we have a part to play, God wants us to participate in His plan. We are all a part of the Body of Christ and we are here to do God's will on the earth today.

God has a plan for our lives, and it is good to know that God has given us His Word and He has sent us the Holy Spirit to guide us and help us find and fulfill His plan. Some people make it seem that it is so hard to know what the will of God is, but through the Word and the Holy Spirit, God will help us to see what His will is, and He will show us how we can accomplish it.

Colossians 1:9-11 (NKJV)
9 For this reason we also, since the day we heard it, do not cease to pray for you, and to ask that you may be filled with the knowledge of His will in all wisdom and spiritual understanding;

10 that you may walk worthy of the Lord, fully pleasing Him, being fruitful in every good work and increasing in the knowledge of God;

11 strengthened with all might, according to His glorious power, for all patience and longsuffering with joy;

This prayer that we find in Colossians 1, which Paul prayed for the people in the church at Colosse, is one of my favorite parts of one of my favorite books of the Bible. I like how Paul not only prayed that the people would know the will of God, but Paul also prayed that they would have wisdom and spiritual understanding about how to do the will of God.

It is one thing to know what to do, but it can be an entirely different thing to know how and when to do what needs to be done. If we want to succeed, we need to have God's timing and methods for His plan.

This is where a lot of people make mistakes. People often have some idea about what God wants them to do and they just assume that God's plan will happen in the next five minutes. One thing I have learned, and we can see in the Bible as well, is that God's plan will often be revealed to us some time before it comes to pass.

For example, David was anointed to be the King of Israel years before it happened. Joseph had a dream of his family bowing down to him, and this did not come to pass right away. In fact, Joseph got in trouble because he talked about his dream too soon.

This is something I have seen in my own life as well. People have asked me, how did you become a teacher at Rhema? How is it that you travel to so many places to teach in Bible schools and churches?

Sometimes people have the idea that what took a process of years in my life to develop somehow happened overnight. The things I do today were really years in the making.

In Colossians 1:9, we can see that God wants us to know His will, with wisdom and spiritual understanding. Then, in Colossians 1:10-11, we see the results of being filled with the knowledge of God's will and having wisdom and spiritual understanding about it.

The results are a life worthy of God, we are fully pleasing to Him, we are fruitful in every good work, we increase in the knowledge of God, and we are strengthened with all might for all patience and longsuffering with joy. All of these things are a result of what we see in Colossians 1:9, being filled with the knowledge of God's will with all wisdom and spiritual understanding.

That seems to be a lot of things that come from knowing and doing the will of God. And that is just it, so many people struggle in so many areas of their life because they do not know the will of God, and if they do, they are often trying to do it in their own understanding based on their own wisdom.

It says in Colossians 1:10, "that you may walk worthy of the Lord". Well, how else would you have a walk, a life, that is worthy of God? How can you live a life that is not only worthy of God, and the price He paid for us through Jesus, and "fully please Him", if it is not by carrying out the will of God?

Too many believers are living their own kind of life, which may be pleasing to them, but it is not part of God's plan and it may not be so pleasing to Him. Certainly, God loves us the way we are, but why stay the way we are if we can improve, why not do our best to please Him?

Colossians 1:10 goes on to say, "being fruitful in every good work". That phrase caught my attention one day as I was reading Colossians, and I had the thought, "Could someone do a good work and not be fruitful?".

Could we do the right things and not have the right results?" The answer is yes. You can do something that is good, but if it is done in the wrong way, at the wrong time, or even by the wrong person, it will be of little or no value.

For example, a church is a good thing. But if God did not direct me to start a church and I am only doing it for my own reasons, then that church and I will both struggle.

Or I could do something God did not lead me to do, but He is directing someone else to do it. The other person who is led by God to do that thing will have much more success than I would have because I am doing it separate from the will of God.

Paul goes on in Colossians 1:10-11 showing us more results of knowing God's will, saying "increasing in the knowledge of God; strengthened with all might". That sounds like something everyone would be interested in, increasing in knowledge and strength.

But, have you ever met a Christian who never seemed to grow and develop spiritually, or who seemed chronically weak in their faith? According to what Paul said here, the reason for this is a person not fully following the will of God.

If we are not walking in the will of God, whether intentionally or ignorantly, we are still out of the will of God. This is never a good place to be and we will not prosper in our relationship with God if we are in the wrong position.

Not Quite Right

We don't want to just get close to doing the will of God, we want to know His will and do it. If we are not fully following the will of God in our life, things will not be the way that they should be.

It would be like wearing your shoes on the wrong feet, it's just not quite right. The basic idea is right, and you want to wear the shoes, but because you have not applied the shoes properly you are going to suffer due to your wrong decision.

You can persist in doing things your way, but the longer you wear those shoes on the wrong feet the worse it is going to be. The best thing is just to make the change and put the shoes on the right feet.

We can only increase in the knowledge of God if we are acting on the knowledge of God that we already have. Just as in a school where one level of knowledge is built upon the previous level, God gives us knowledge that will add to what we already know and have working in our life.

If we are not doing anything with what God has given us in the past, then there is not much of a chance that we will increase in our knowledge of God. You can't go to college without going through high school, and you can't go to high school if you did not finish elementary school.

Many believers are really still at the Kindergarten level of spiritual development because they do not spend much, if any time, with God and His Word and they are not putting what they do know into practice, thus they are not increasing in the knowledge of God.

The same is true of being "strengthened with all might", you don't get stronger by doing nothing. You can go to the health club and sit there all day without getting any stronger. If you never do any training for your body it will never develop, you have to do something with what you have to continue to increase in knowledge and strength.

We all want to know the will of God and find His direction for our life, but sometimes this seems like such a difficult process. We want to find the general direction for our life and we need the details about how to do it.

We can see the results of knowing God's will, but how can we know His will? This is the whole point to the teaching I have done on this subject and the reason for this book. God wants us to know and do His will.

First Things First

If we start out with the wrong mentality it will hinder us in following God and His plan for our life. If we are not sure that God wants us to know His will, or if we think our life is just a series of random events that we have no part in, then we will not find and fulfill the will of God, in fact we might not even look for it.

Remember what we just looked at in Colossians 1; Paul, inspired by the Holy Spirit, prayed that those believers would be filled with the knowledge of God's will. How could Paul pray such a prayer if God did not want us to know His will?

Too many times, believers think that God is trying to hide His plan from them. People somehow get the idea that finding the will of God is like winning the lottery, where the odds of success are astronomical.

So many Christians just float from one circumstance to the next without any direction in their life. Some believers just go from one event in life to the next, somehow thinking that this is the way it is supposed to be, drifting from one set of circumstances to the next.

It would be like being on a ship that is being pushed around by the wind with no one trying to direct the ship. If you knew the course you were supposed to take, then you would do what you could to go in that direction and not just hope the wind blows you the right way.

This is the reason that having the right attitude and a proper understanding about God and His plan for our life is so vital. If we somehow think that our life has no purpose, or if we think that for some reason God is hiding His purpose from us, or if we misunderstand how God wants to direct us in our life, we will be like the ship that is just drifting and being pushed around by the wind and the waves.

We need to have a clear understanding of our purpose in life and realize that God wants us to know what that purpose is. This is why having the right mindset is extremely important.

How do we keep moving forward in our relationship with God? How do we deal with questions and difficult situations? This is often when we ask the question, "What do I do now?".

Very often the answer is that no new direction, is direction. That may just sound like gibberish, or something trivial, but it is still true. If we do not have some new direction in our life, then we need to keep on going in the direction we are currently going. And by doing this we will continue moving forward in God's plan and we will get to the place where we need to be.

This truth is something that I learned in my own life. There were some areas in my life that I was talking to God about, and I was looking for some specific steps to take, I wanted to know what to do, I wanted to know the will of God and how to fulfill it.

What I realized was that I had the problem of looking past where I was, and what I was supposed to be doing, and I was trying to find something new. Too often we think we need something new and different when we already have something as valuable as what we are looking for.

We sometimes try to look too far ahead to steps we think we might take in the future, instead of just taking the step or steps that we can take right now. Instead of looking three or four steps ahead to figure out what to do then, we need to take the step we have now. Often, we will find that if we will just take the step we have now, that then more steps will be seen.

In any situation where we are moving forward, whether going up a set of stairs or walking straight ahead, we need to focus on the step we are taking. If we try to skip steps, or we are not paying attention to the step we are taking, it is easy to have a problem.

In my situation, my thinking was that God would tell me to do this or that, to go here or there, or maybe to change something in my life. Instead, what God talked to me about, over and over, was that I needed to continue doing what I was doing.

That is when I realized that no new direction, is direction. But that means we at least have some current direction in our life about what we need to do and where we need to go.

So, how do we learn what that direction is? The first step is to go to the Bible, what does God's Word have to say? This is the first step in finding God's will for our life and the first step we should always take.

2. What Does God's Word Say?

The first place we need to look for any answers, wisdom, or direction that we need in life, is God's Word, the Bible. It is true that we are led by the Holy Spirit, which is something we will look at later, but God has given us His Word to help direct us.

A good question to ask ourselves is, what has God shown me in His Word? What do I already know? When we are looking for direction and answers, we too often minimize what God has to say to us in His Word.

So often we spend time looking for something new, or looking at what we don't know and we don't have. But we first need to focus on and then do what God has told us.

Deuteronomy 29:29 (NKJV)
29 "The secret things belong to the LORD our God, but those things which are revealed belong to us and to our children forever, that we may do all the words of this law.

This verse shows us a major principle that will help us in our life, we must focus on and do what God has told us. There are some things we do not know, there are some things we do not understand, but there are some things we do know and understand. If we already know something that we need to do, then we should just do it.

In the original Hebrew, the word "secret" in Deuteronomy 29:29 is talking about things that are hidden, something we do not know. Many times, I have met people who are trying to figure out something that they do not know or understand, and they are neglecting what they already know and do understand. We can and should work with what we have.

We must focus on what has been revealed to us and not be so concerned about what we don't know. It is easy to wonder about why something happened, or didn't happen, and endlessly ponder things we may never understand.

The way I have learned to look at things like this is that if God wants me to know something, then He will tell me about it. God is far wiser than any human being and He knows what we need to know and when we need to know it.

We can get caught up in curiosity, wondering about all kinds of things, but if we first focus on what God has already told us, what He has already revealed to us, and do those things, then we will be going in the right direction.

We need to focus on what we do know. As it has been said, "If you don't know, you can't go". If you are at a loss for which direction to go, then you usually don't go anywhere.

James 1:21-22 (NKJV)
21 Therefore lay aside all filthiness and overflow of wickedness, and receive with meekness the implanted word, which is able to save your souls.
22 But be doers of the word, and not hearers only, deceiving yourselves.

You could say that these verses in James are the New Testament equivalent of Deuteronomy 29:29. We need to be people who do what the Word of God tells us to do.

If we do not do what God has told us to do, we are deceiving ourselves. When God shows us something, we need to do it and make it a part of our life. In James 1:25 it goes on to say that those who do what the Word says are those who are blessed.

We need to realize that our life as a Christian and our relationship with God is a journey we take for our entire life, what we are doing is not just trying to go from blessing to blessing, or to get to a certain goal or destination. The principles we see in God's Word need to be the basis for our life.

The Bible is not some recipe book that we look in to find some specific formula to use in some situation. Too often we are only interested in doing what the Word says if we see some goal at the end of the process; sometimes we are only willing to do what

God has told us to do if we believe it will get us where we want to go.

Doing what God says in His Word should be our lifestyle, not just a process we go through as a means to an end. Sometimes our mentality is that we are doing what needs to be done just so we can achieve some goal and reach the end of the process.

Many times, what we all fail to do is recognize that we not only need to do what God has told us to do now, but we need to keep on doing it. We don't just pray and talk to God when there is a crisis, and we don't just build up our faith for healing, finances, or direction when we are specifically in need of those things.

For The Rest Of Your Life

James 1:25 (NKJV)
25 But he who looks into the perfect law of liberty and continues in it, and is not a forgetful hearer

but a doer of the work, this one will be blessed in what he does.

Years ago, I talked to someone about a situation they were dealing with. We talked about what the Bible says and I encouraged this person to focus on, think about, do, and speak God's Word. The person then asked me, "How long do I need to do this?" My response was, "For the rest of your life".

No matter what situation we are in, God's Word has the answer, and not just for that moment. God's Word gives us answers that we can use, and should use, for the rest of our life! We need to do what we know to do, and keep on doing it.

This is not only how we reach the goal we are pursuing, or find the answers that we need, but it is also how we live our life and develop in our relationship with God. We should focus on doing the will of God as a part of our life, not just as some formula for success.

When God was helping me to understand this truth of no new direction is direction, I was reading and studying the Word as well as talking to God about what to do next in my life. Again, and again, God would remind me of things I already knew and that were already working in my life.

God reminded me of those things, and rather than giving me some new steps to take, He encouraged me to just keep doing what I was already doing. When I was looking for something new, some specific step to take, something different to do, His reply was for me to keep on doing what I was already doing!

At first, this bothered me, and I did the same thing I mentioned before, I kept trying to figure out the things I did not understand or know about. My focus was not on doing what I already knew to do, I wanted to know something else, something new and different, that I thought would help me get where I needed to go.

What I did not realize at the time was that there was more to do with the things that I already knew, and I was really not ready for anything new at that time. As we learn the Word and then we do what the Word tells us, we are developing spiritually.

For example, maybe we are studying about righteousness. The more we study that subject the more developed we are in that truth. There is no overdevelopment spiritually, and there is room for all of us to grow.

We sometimes fail to realize how much room we have to grow spiritually. We can think we are at a point where we need to move forward in some things, but God knows that we need to stay right where we are, doing what we are already doing, to develop more in a certain truth, or in our ability to do something better than we have done it before.

We may be looking for direction about what to do next in the wrong place. Many times, what we need to do has already been revealed to us in

God's Word, and we just need to keep on doing those things we already know to do.

God may have more work to do in us where we are at right now before we move forward in His plan. There may be more for us to learn as we apply what we already know about God's Word in our life.

We may be looking for something new when we just need to do what we already know to do. We will never get to the point of walking in perfect harmony with the Word of God. We are still human and limited, which means there will always be areas where we can grow and develop spiritually.

Sometimes God will keep us in one place, so to speak, doing the same things to develop something in us that He knows we will need in the future. We may not understand that completely yet, but He does, and we need to listen to His direction.

A Light In The Dark

Psalm 119:130 (NKJV)
130 The entrance of Your words gives light; It gives understanding to the simple.

Most people have had the unfortunate experience of bumping into something in the dark. Why did that happen? It was because they could not see where they were going.

God's Word gives us light and understanding, God's Word helps us to see where we need to go. Sometimes we *only* want to rely on being led by the Holy Spirit, but God will also guide us through His Word.

God's Word is what God has said, and is saying, to us, so it is valuable for us to know what His Word says. We need to learn to let God's Word guide us in life. And the Holy Spirit will never lead us contrary to God's Word, so the Bible is always a good place to start in finding direction for our life.

If there is an area in our lives where we have questions, then that is an area where we are in the dark. Our answer is to go to God's Word to get the light that we need for the situation we are in. It may just come down to the fact that we want God to speak to us and just give us the answer, we don't want to take the time necessary to get into God's Word to find the light that we need.

If you are in the dark, even a small amount of light can help you see where you are and where you need to go. It is amazing what a little light can do for us in a dark situation.

You can see a lot in a dark room with just the light that comes through under the door. You might wish you had a spotlight to really see what is around you and what direction to go, but with just a little light you can see a lot.

The same is true with God's Word. Sometimes people think that they need to be something like a Bible scholar to be able to deal with all of the issues of life. The truth is that God's Word gives us light, all of God's Word will do that for us, even one verse can give us the light we need for our situation.

A Lamp And A Light

Psalm 119:105 (NKJV)
105 Your word is a lamp to my feet and a light to my path.

David understood that God's Word gives us light to live our life in the best possible way. David realized that by following the precepts of what God had said he would be following God, because God and His Word are one.

One of my favorite subjects to teach about is being led by the Holy Spirit, this is how God wants to lead His children (Romans 8:14). But, something that I always stress is how we so often underestimate the value of God's Word when it comes to following God's direction for our life.

If we want to know how to be successful in life, we need to follow the Word. If we want to have wisdom to deal with the challenges that we face, we need to follow the Word. If we want an understanding on how to successfully deal with people, we need to follow the teaching we have in the Word.

God has given us His Word to help us in every area of our life. God's Word gives us the wisdom we need to be able to successfully navigate our way through life, no matter what may come.

Yes, as I mentioned before, the Holy Spirit will lead us and direct us in life; and again, this is something we will look at later in this book. But we need to realize that God can and will give us light and direction through His Word. We don't want to put an emphasis on following the Holy Spirit without realizing that the Word and the Spirit work together.

We are sometimes looking everywhere imaginable for direction from God when the most obvious source of direction and wisdom from God, the Bible, is right at our fingertips. Thank God for the Holy Spirit, but thank God for His Word and the light it gives to us.

When we are looking for direction in our life, when we have a question, when we need wisdom about how to deal with a situation, when we have an area of lack in our life, our first place to go should always be God's Word. In every situation, we need to always ask ourselves, "What does God's Word say about this?", that is how we will live a life of success in doing the will of God.

More Than We Know

We sometimes have the idea that we need more revelation from God's Word than we really do. The thing is that we sometimes don't realize how much room we have to grow and develop in the things that we already know. This again is how the idea of no new direction is direction fits in.

Too often we are looking for new things when we have not even made full use of the things we already have and know. There is no such thing as overdevelopment in our understanding and use of God's Word, and we will never get to the point where we have too much of God's Word in our life.

One good example of this is what we see in 1 Corinthians 13, especially in verses four through the beginning of verse eight. This is where it talks about the love of God and what it looks like.

1 Corinthians 13:4-8a (NKJV)
4 Love suffers long and is kind; love does not envy; love does not parade itself, is not puffed up;
5 does not behave rudely, does not seek its own, is not provoked, thinks no evil;
6 does not rejoice in iniquity, but rejoices in the truth;
7 bears all things, believes all things, hopes all things, endures all things.
8 Love never fails. ...

The area of the love of God is one we will always need some development in. No matter what the future holds, and what plan God has for our life, we will need to be as developed as we possibly can be in the love of God.

Romans 5:5 (NKJV)
5 Now hope does not disappoint, because the love of God has been poured out in our hearts by the Holy Spirit who was given to us.

In Romans 5:5 it tells us that the love of God is already in our hearts, and 1 Corinthians 13 tells what this love looks like. We have the love of God in us, but is our life a display of the love of God to everyone we meet?

Is there more growth and development available to us in this area? Certainly there is, which is why when it seems that we don't have any new direction or revelation from God in our life, we need to continue doing what it is we know to do and develop in that.

It is important to realize that there are things we are doing today that we need more development in, so that we will be able to successfully move forward in God's plan for our life. We are sometimes in a hurry to take the next step in what God has for us, not realizing that we may not be completely ready for what lies ahead.

Many Christians have taken steps forward, to do what God has called them to do, and then they have stumbled due to a lack of spiritual maturity in their life. Sometimes the direction we need has already been given to us in God's Word, and we need to keep on doing what God has already told us to do.

If God has not given us any "new" direction, then we need to continue going with whatever direction that He has already given to us through His Word. But we know that is not all.

Thank God for His Word and thank God for the leading of the Holy Spirit! God has given us His Holy Spirit to help guide us in life.

3. What Has The Holy Spirit Said?

When people are seeking direction in their life, they often look in the wrong place. Part of the answer to the question of, "What do I do now?" is that no new direction is direction, and that many times we already know something we can and should be doing.

This is true with what we see in the Bible, and it is also true in our being led by the Holy Spirit. If we have seen something in the Word of God that we can do, we should do it. And, if the Holy Spirit is leading us to do something, then we should do that.

To learn about being led by the Holy Spirit, we have to understand some basic things. One amazing basic fact that we don't always understand as we should is that God, through the Holy Spirit, is living inside of us.

1 Corinthians 3:16 (NKJV)
16 Do you not know that you are the temple of God and that the Spirit of God dwells in you?

When we received Jesus as our Lord and Savior, the Holy Spirit came to make His home in us. So, why is He there? What is the Holy Spirit doing in us? Is He just floating around, riding along through life in our body? No, He is in us to help us and guide us in our life.

John 14:26 (NKJV)
26 But the Helper, the Holy Spirit, whom the Father will send in My name, He will teach you all things, and bring to your remembrance all things that I said to you.

Jesus said He would send us the Helper, the Holy Spirit. Jesus said that the Holy Spirit would teach us all things, which would include what to do in our life, and even how to do what needs to be done.

God has given us the Holy Spirit to help give us the direction that we need in life, and to do the things that God has called us to do. Sadly, many Christians go through the majority of their life not really understanding that God is trying to lead them by the Holy Spirit.

Many people have wrong ideas about who the Holy Spirit is and how He wants to operate in our life. If we do not correctly understand what the Holy Spirit can do, then any help we might receive from Him would be minimal, at best.

Some Christians have no real idea what the role of the Holy Spirit is in the life of the Christian, while others might place an overemphasis on the Holy Spirit and the part He should play in our life, because they ignore how God will lead us through His Word. We need to know exactly what role the Holy Spirit should have in the life of a believer.

Led By The Spirit Of God

Romans 8:14-16 (NKJV)
14 For as many as are led by the Spirit of God, these are sons of God.

15 For you did not receive the spirit of bondage again to fear, but you received the Spirit of adoption by whom we cry out, "Abba, Father."
16 The Spirit Himself bears witness with our spirit that we are children of God,

God's plan is for each and every one of His children to be led by the Holy Spirit. Christians are not led by voices, open or closed doors, circumstances, or by other Christians.

Christians, because they have the Holy Spirit living in them, are supposed to be guided in life by that same Holy Spirit. Romans 8 not only tells us that as children of God we are supposed to be led by the Holy Spirit, but it even shows us how this works.

Being led by the Holy Spirit is not as big of a mystery as some people make it out to be. Again, because we sometimes have a misunderstanding about how the Holy Spirit will work in our life, we struggle in the area of finding and following God's direction.

Romans 8:14 says we are led by the Holy Spirit, and then in Romans 8:16 it shows us one of the main ways that works in our life: "*The Spirit Himself bears witness with our spirit that we are children of God*". This is a big part of how the Holy Spirit leads us, and understanding this principle will be a big help to us.

What does it mean that the Holy Spirit will bear witness with our spirit, how is this supposed to work? The words "bears witness with" in Romans 8:16 can also be translated as "to testify jointly".

We could rephrase that verse this way: "The Holy Spirit and our spirit testify jointly that we are children of God". Another way to say it would be that the Holy Spirit and our spirit have the same testimony.

If someone is a witness to something, they tell what they know, they explain what they have seen, they give their testimony. If you have two people who say the same thing about what they are a witness to, then there is agreement in what they have said, their witness is the same, they are bearing witness together, they are testifying jointly.

When you become a new creation in Christ, you have a confirmation of it in your spirit, your inner man. You know on the inside that you have been born again; your spirit and the Holy Spirit bear witness together.

You don't know you are born again because someone else told you about it, you don't know it because of some physical, or even mental evidence, but you have an inner knowing about it. That is what it means that the Holy Spirit bears witness with our spirit.

In Romans 7:22 it talks about "the inward man", in Ephesians 3:16 it talks about "the inner man", and in 1 Peter 3:4 it talks about "the hidden person of the heart". All of these terms are talking about the spirit of man, the part of us that is changed at salvation into a "new creation in Christ" (2 Corinthians 5:17). This is the part of man that is in

contact with God, the part of us that can
agreement with the Holy Spirit. Christi
look for direction from God in every plac
where they should be looking, to their spirit.

Proverbs 20:27 says that the spirit of man is the lamp of the Lord. A lamp gives us light and helps us to see what we need to see. In a spiritual sense, God will give us light to see and know what we need to do in our spirit.

Proverbs 20:27 helps us to understand that God is going to give us direction in our spirit and not through our mind or body. We cannot base God's direction for our life on how we feel, physically or emotionally, and we cannot base God's direction for our life on what we think. We base God's direction for our life on the leading of the Holy Spirit in our spirit.

Let Peace Rule

To better understand what it means for the Holy Spirit to bear witness with our spirit, we can look at another verse related to this. Rather than just go by someone's experience of being led by the Holy Spirit, it is better to see what God's Word has to say about it.

Colossians 3:15 (NKJV)
15 And let the peace of God rule in your hearts, to which also you were called in one body; and be thankful.

If two people were to give the same testimony about something, then there is agreement about it, and where there is agreement there is peace. If there is no agreement about something, then there is no peace.

One simple way to better understand the Holy Spirit bearing witness with our spirit is by the presence of peace. Before we receive Jesus as our Lord and Savior, there is no agreement, no peace, between our spirit and the Holy Spirit.

For example, when I understood my need to receive Jesus as my Savior, I remember that it seemed like someone turned up the heat and I somehow became very uncomfortable. What was happening? My spirit and the Holy Spirit were not agreeing about my spiritual position, I was spiritually separated from God and there was no peace in my "inner man".

Then, when I received Jesus, I remember that while there were no flashing lights or even some big emotional feeling, I still knew something was different. For the first time I had real peace in my heart.

Before salvation, I was an unhappy person with a generally negative view of life. Once I became a Christian, things changed, there was something different on the inside of me.

Now, I am not saying that my life completely turned around the moment I was saved, changes in my life took some spiritual growth and development over time. But there was an element of peace I had never experienced before. There was an agreement with my spirit and the Holy Spirit that I was indeed a child of God!

As Romans 8:16 says, the Holy Spirit bears witness with our spirit that we are a child of God, there is peace in our heart. Colossians 3:15 shows us this same principle by telling us we need to allow the peace of God to rule in our heart. We need to look for that inner peace from God, that witness of the Holy Spirit in our spirit to follow God's direction in our life.

This is where the no new direction is direction idea comes in. As long as we are in a place where we have peace in our heart, as long as we have been following the direction of the Holy Spirit, we stay in that place until we have new direction from God by the Holy Spirit.

For example, if I have sensed a prompting from the Holy Spirit to do a certain type of ministry, or to get involved working with the children's ministry in the church, or serving as an usher, or helping to clean in the church, or doing something else, then I get involved in that thing and I keep on doing it until God gives me further direction.

It can very well be that God has directed me to do one of these things for some amount of time, because there is something there I need to learn, or someone I need to connect with, or something already in my life that needs to be developed for me to go to another level in my relationship with God. This is why we don't just start moving from one thing to another thinking that this is the way to find new direction from God.

This is where people sometimes have a problem. They are involved somewhere in their local church, and everything is fine, but because nothing has changed lately, they think they need to do something else, or go somewhere else. People keep thinking they need to change something externally when really God is trying to work on something with them internally, He is working on their spiritual development.

If we are in a situation where we are serving God and others and we have peace in our heart, then we don't need to start looking around for something else! We need to keep being faithful doing what we are doing, right where we are, and trust God to give us new direction when we need it.

He Will Let You Know

Philippians 3:14-15 (NKJV)
14 I press toward the goal for the prize of the upward call of God in Christ Jesus.
15 Therefore let us, as many as are mature, have this mind; and if in anything you think otherwise, God will reveal even this to you.

This verse in Philippians 3 has been a big help to me in following God's direction in my life. Paul is talking about moving toward the goal of the "upward call" of God, he is speaking about doing the will of God.

Paul is talking about moving forward in God's plan, and in verse 15 he says that this is how the mature believers ought to think, and this is what they need to focus on. What Paul says next helps me to be at peace, when I feel like I need to do something different or change something in my life, even though God has not given me any new direction.

Paul says that while the mature believers needs to think this way, even if we are thinking differently, even if we are not doing something right, or going in the right direction, God will reveal this to us! God is not trying to hide His plan from us, He wants us to know His will.

We saw earlier in Colossians 1:9 how Paul was praying for the believers in Colosse to be filled with the knowledge of God's will, in all wisdom and spiritual understanding. Paul was certainly not praying contrary to the will of God, in fact Paul was inspired by the Holy Spirit to pray what he was praying.

We need to follow the leading of the Holy Spirit, looking for the peace of God and then letting it rule in our hearts, no matter how things look, or how we "feel" naturally. No one knows the plan of God for our life better than God and we need to follow His direction.

If the Holy Spirit has directed us to do something, and He has led us to a certain place or to do a certain thing, then we need to stay in that place being faithful to do that thing until God lets us know it is time to move on. God is not going to let us just sit around, wasting our time doing the wrong thing. If we are not in the right place and doing the thing that God wants us to do, He will reveal that to us!

As long as our heart's desire is to follow God and do His will, we can be sure that He will speak to us through His Word and by the Holy Spirit to show us what to do. God knows how to get through to us and He will make His will known to us.

We think of the plan of God for our life in relation to how it will benefit us. We normally just think about what will happen to us and for us if we do the things that God calls us to do.

But God sees things differently than we do. God sees the blessings that will come to us as a result of our doing His will, but God also knows that others will be blessed when we obey the things that He calls us to do. God does not want us to sit idly by while His plan and purpose for our life, as a part of His overall plan for the world, is left undone.

The key for us is that when we do know we need to do something that we go ahead and do it. Then we stay faithful in that place until God moves us onward. This is where no new direction is direction. If the Holy Spirit is not showing us a new step to take, then we need to stay where we are, doing what we know to do now, until further direction is given.

The Holy Spirit will guide us in all of the details of life. The question is, do we spend time listening to Him and learning to recognize His voice? This can be a big reason that God will have us in sort of a holding pattern until it is time for us to move forward. God will teach us and train us to develop in doing His will by helping us to become more sensitive to His voice right where we are, as we do what He has called us to do.

Sometimes people say to me, "Jim, I don't know what God wants me to do and I am so frustrated!". I understand that completely as I have been there before myself. But, what has God's Word told us to do and what has the Holy Spirit led us to do?

The truth is that we always know something we can do where we are now. This is how we get to the place we need to be and find the answers that we seek, we continue doing what we know to do now.

Even if it seems like the Holy Spirit has not said anything to us, we can always go back to God's Word to see what it says. If we have some direction, through the Word or by the Spirit, then we need to keep going that direction.

There were many times I heard even Brother Hagin say, "I go as much by what God doesn't say as by what He does say". This is true for every believer, if God says something, then do it. But if God does not say anything, then we need to do what we already know to do.

The Word And The Spirit Agree

We can, and should, always start with the general will of God for our lives as it is revealed to us in the Bible. In the Bible we can learn all about how God wants us to live and how to properly serve Him, in a general sense. Then the Holy Spirit can direct us specifically as to how we should carry out God's general will and put His Word into practice in our individual lives.

Sometimes Christians get in trouble because they believe the Holy Spirit is leading them to do something that is not in agreement with what is found in the Bible. The truth is that the Holy Spirit will never lead us contrary to what God has said in His Word, and why would He? Why would God give us His Word, as revealed to us in the Bible, and then lead us by His Spirit to do something opposite of what the Bible says?

2 Peter 1:20-21 (NKJV)
20 knowing this first, that no prophecy of Scripture is of any private interpretation,
21 for prophecy never came by the will of man, but holy men of God spoke as they were moved by the Holy Spirit.

Peter shows us how that nothing in Scripture is of a private interpretation, it is not something that just came from some man. Holy men of God spoke, and wrote, as they were moved by the Holy Spirit, as the Holy Spirit guided them.

What we have in the Scriptures came from God to men by the direction of the Holy Spirit, and God is not going to disagree with Himself! This is why the Bible is so important for us, even in being led by the Holy Spirit. We can always check any leading or direction we have with what we find in God's Word.

There are people who will tell you that the Holy Spirit may reveal new things to us today, and not all the truth from God is in the Bible, and things like that. This is a very dangerous position to take. If we cannot trust the Bible, how can we trust some "leading" that disagrees with what has been the standard for believers for nearly 2,000 years?

Of course, the Holy Spirit will lead us and guide us to do things not specifically mentioned in the Scriptures, like in my case of moving to Oklahoma to attend Rhema Bible Training College, or moving to Europe to teach in Bible schools and churches. But those things are all found in principle in the Bible, so it is easy to see that they are biblical steps of direction from God.

God wants us to know His will, and He wants us to learn to be led by His Spirit, and this is sometimes the reason we are in one "place" for a certain period of time. God is developing us in this area, and as we move forward in His plan it can, and most likely will, be even more important to know and recognize His leading in our life.

4. What Opportunities Do You Have?

When talking about finding God's direction for our life, the two areas we looked at of finding God's will in His Word and being led by the Holy Spirit are the main areas that people will always talk about. This is good and right, because knowing God's Word and allowing the Holy Spirit to direct us are keys to finding and fulfilling God's plan for our life.

But, while these are the two main ways that God will direct us, there is something else I have seen in my own life, and in the lives of others, that fits in here. It is how God will use opportunities we are presented with, to guide us into His will and plan for our life.

Taking advantage of opportunities may seem like a strange thing to bring up in talking about finding God's will, but it is actually a very important part of learning to follow God and discover His plan for our life. This does not take anything away from God's Word or the leading of the Holy Spirit, but it is something that works along with them.

As we are a doer of the Word, and listen to the direction of the Holy Spirit, we will find opportunities in our life to put into practice what we know. But because this is an area that people often don't understand, we sometime fail to take advantage of the godly opportunities we are presented with.

The thing is that so often we are mainly looking at what we don't know or don't have and we spend an excessive amount of time wondering about that. Instead, we need to ask ourselves, "What opportunities has God given to me, what can I do where I am at right now?".

Where It All Begins

No matter where we are now, naturally or spiritually, there is something we can do. This is where it all begins, doing what we can do right now and being faithful in doing it.

God will give us opportunities to do things, as a part of His will for our life, that will help us to grow and develop, as well as prepare us for the things that are yet to come. Very often people miss the opportunities that God puts right in front of them, because they are looking two or three steps down the road to something else that they think God may want them to do.

But, are we supposed to just get involved in any and every opportunity that comes our way? Do we just expect every open door and opportunity that we come across to be part of God's plan? How exactly does this work where opportunities can be a vital part of the process in our life of finding and fulfilling the will of God?

We are not just led by opportunities, and sometimes even what looks right is the wrong thing for us to do. Also, just because something is right, and we could do it, does not mean that we are the person who is supposed to do it.

But, by correctly taking advantage of the opportunities that God brings to us, we can develop in learning how to listen to the direction of the Holy

Spirit and in how we act on God's Word. We need to know the Word of God and understand the leading of the Holy Spirit in our life. It is a combination of the Word and the Spirit, as well as the things we do, that will help us move forward in the plan and purpose God has for us.

Start With What You Know

There is a story in Acts 16 about Paul and his companions that is a great example of taking advantage of the opportunities we have, and being led by the Holy Spirit. We can look at what Paul did in his situation to learn what we can do in our own lives.

Acts 16:6-10 (NKJV)
6 Now when they had gone through Phrygia and the region of Galatia, they were forbidden by the Holy Spirit to preach the word in Asia.
7 After they had come to Mysia, they tried to go into Bithynia, but the Spirit did not permit them.
8 So passing by Mysia, they came down to Troas.
9 And a vision appeared to Paul in the night. A man

of Macedonia stood and pleaded with him, saying, "Come over to Macedonia and help us."
10 Now after he had seen the vision, immediately we sought to go to Macedonia, concluding that the Lord had called us to preach the gospel to them.

First of all, Paul understood God's plan for his life. Paul knew that God wanted him to go and preach the Gospel message; that was the basic, general will of God for Paul's life, just like it is for us.

We can read that Paul and his group were "forbidden" to preach the Word in Asia. That seems a bit strange, doesn't it? They were forbidden to preach the Word! How can that be?

Preaching God's Word, sharing the Gospel message, is a good thing, isn't it? Remember how in chapter two we talked about the prayer in Colossians 1? It talked about being fruitful in every good work, and I pointed out that even if we do a good thing, but God did not lead us to do it, we will be unfruitful in that thing.

It was the will of God for Paul to preach the Gospel, but not in that place at that time. Then, in verse 7, Paul and his group tried to go to another place, and again the Holy Spirit, "did not permit them". These verses can be a bit perplexing, especially if we don't understand how God will lead and guide us today.

Often people think that if something is good, then they should just automatically do it. Something like preaching the Gospel is a good thing, but again, notice that by the direction of the Holy Spirit, God was not allowing them to do that, in that place and at that time.

Just like Paul, we can start out with the basic will of God, as we find it in the Bible, and then move forward from there. But just because we see something that is good to do does not mean that it is our job to do it. That may sound contradictory or confusing, but it really isn't.

Paul and his group knew the basic will of God and they had the possibility, the opportunity, to preach the Word of God in these places. But even though this was a good thing to do, it was not the thing for Paul and his group to do in that place at that time.

Paul started with what he knew he was supposed to do, preach the Gospel. Paul then took a step in the will of God that he knew, where there was an opportunity, and all the while I believe that he was checking for the peace of God in his heart, the witness of the Holy Spirit.

It says that the Holy Spirit forbid them and would not permit them to preach the Gospel in those places. How did that work? While we are not told specifically, I believe that Paul, and possibly others in his group, could sense that once they started to go in those different directions that there was no peace, no witness of the Spirit, so they did not go.

Then what did they do? After things did not work out the first time (verse 6), they tried another step in the general will of God (verse 7), there was another place they could go, there was another opportunity. But that was not the right direction either.

However, Paul and his group did not just give up, they used what they knew as their starting point, while always looking for the witness of the Holy Spirit, and kept moving forward, doing what they could to take advantage of the opportunities they had to do the will of God. They knew that there were a couple of places that they could not go, so they looked to go somewhere else.

They were looking for opportunities to do what they knew was right to do, while following the direction of the Holy Spirit. This is the same way it will work in our lives, and this is a way that God will help us develop in being led by the Holy Spirit and following His plan for our life.

Then, in verse 8, it says they passed by the city of Mysia, where they had been before, and came to the city of Troas. This is where Paul had the vision of the man of Macedonia. As Paul and his group kept looking to take advantage of opportunities to do what they knew to do, God gave them the direction that they needed.

This is a simple example of how to find the will of God for our life. First, we find out what is right by seeing what God's Word has to say, and then we let the Holy Spirit direct us in how those things should work in our life. Second, we look for opportunities to do those good things that we know are right to do. Third, we follow the direction of the Holy Spirit about how, when, and even if we should do those things.

This is the basic place for all of us to start. The point is that, like Paul, we need to know the basics of what we can and should do, and we let the Holy Spirit direct us from there. Then, once we have direction from the Holy Spirit, we keep going that direction and keep doing what we are led to do until we are led to do something else.

Step By Step

There is a simple process I have learned that helped me determine whether or not many of the opportunities that I have had are the right opportunities for me. As I have put these simple principles into action, it has been a great help to me, and I am sure it will be to you as well.

First of all, when I am presented with an opportunity to do something, I check what I know from God's Word. Is this opportunity a good Bible-based thing? If the answer to this is yes, then I can go a step further and determine if I am actually able to do that thing and I have the time for it.

For example, many years ago when I was living in Oklahoma, someone invited me to a prayer meeting. Well, I know prayer is a good thing, I can pray, and I also did not have some other commitment that would stop me from going to the prayer meeting I was invited to.

The next thing in this process was that I checked to see if there was something from the Holy Spirit where it seemed as though, for whatever reason, I should not go; sometimes people refer to this as a "check" in their spirit, a sort of don't go signal, like Paul had. But I had a peace in my heart about it and so I went to the prayer meeting.

Now, here is the interesting part of the story. The prayer meeting was being conducted by some people who were involved in some ministry in Europe, and it was a prayer meeting for Europe!

At the time I had no real interest in missions, and moving to Europe for ministry was probably the furthest thing from my mind. But, to make a long story short, it was through these prayer meetings that I met several people that I am now connected with and work with in Europe.

What if I had not taken advantage of that opportunity? What if I had said, "Well, prayer is fine, but I am not interested in Europe so I'll just stay home and read a book or something", what would have happened then? I would have missed a great opportunity to connect with some people that I needed to be connected with.

If I had only tried to figure this out in my mind, I would have missed a good opportunity that I believe God brought my way. It was a good, Bible-based thing to do and I had peace in my heart about it, so I went and it really changed my life.

Ephesians 2:8-10 (NKJV)
8 For by grace you have been saved through faith, and that not of yourselves; it is the gift of God,
9 not of works, lest anyone should boast.
10 For we are His workmanship, created in Christ Jesus for good works, which God prepared beforehand that we should walk in them.

Salvation is the beginning of our relationship with God, our first step in God's plan. We are saved by grace through faith, not based on our works but based on the work that was done by Jesus.

From the point of our being born again and becoming a new creation in Christ, we begin to step into the plan of God for our life. However, our first step out of the kingdom of darkness into the Kingdom of Light should not be our last step.

And, we don't want to skip steps in the will of God, because every step is important. We are not the best judge of what things or steps are important and which are not. God is a much better judge of that, and we need to follow Him and let Him guide us step by step into what He has prepared for us.

Ephesians 2:10 shows us that we are God's workmanship, His creation. And He has created us for a purpose. God has a plan and a purpose for each of us, and from the beginning of time He has had this purpose in mind; we need to learn what that purpose is.

One of the greatest goals of the believer is to discover their God given purpose in life. What is it that God created me to do, what is His purpose for my life? One way that we learn this is through experience.

What people do not realize is that while we may not be called to do some things, and we may not have a direct leading from the Holy Spirit to do something, that doesn't mean that we cannot or should not do it. And, rather than hindering us from fulfilling God's plan for our life, by doing things we may not ultimately be called to do, we can actually prepare ourselves to do the will of God.

Some people are sitting around waiting for something that they believe they should be doing to happen, not realizing that if they started doing that thing right now, they would not really be prepared to do it. This is why we will sometimes find opportunities to do some things that we are not specifically called to do; God is using these opportunities to prepare us.

Preparation Time Is Never Wasted Time

When I attended Rhema Bible Training College I had some wonderful teachers that helped me to learn more about God, His Word, and how to do what God has called me to do. One teacher I had was named Keith Moore, and he had a saying that, "Preparation time is never wasted time".

That is a great statement, and one truth in it is that preparation time never ends. However, we often don't really understand this. We often just think about some goal that we are trying to reach or some place that we want to get to. The things we are doing now can help us to develop spiritually to be ready for the things that are still to come.

We are sometimes too quick to try and move on from where we are now, to what we believe, or hope to be, the next thing in our life. We often fail to realize that what we do now is always preparation for what is yet to come, and sometimes we need more time to prepare where we are right now than we might think.

But, if we will be patient, and allow God to work in our life, He will move us on when the time is right, and when He knows that we have received all the training and preparation we need where we are now, to be ready for what will come next. We certainly don't want to be in the situation where God is ready to move us forward and we are not prepared to do what He is calling us to do.

What opportunities have come into your life? What can you do right now, where you are, with what you have? If we will take advantage of what we can do now and be faithful at it we will very often find later on that those things are the exact things that God has used to prepare us for what He has called us to do.

5. What Should I Do Now?

Once we learn something, or even get a better understanding of it, we then need to act on it and put it into practice. After all of the things we have looked at in this book, it would be good to ask the question, what should I do now?

But a better question we could ask is, what are we currently doing? What do you know from God's Word that you can put into practice? What direction has God given you by the Holy Spirit, and are you following that direction? What opportunities do you have? Have you taken advantage of those opportunities and are you doing them faithfully?

Like many people, I had the same hindrance, I thought that I had to get some great revelation from God's Word, see an angel, or hear a voice from heaven before I got started doing something for God. Like many people, I did not want to get stuck doing something that did not fit what I was so sure that God was calling me to do.

But the real truth is, as we have already stated, we need to start where we are, doing what we can do. When it seems like we have no new direction, then we need to keep on faithfully doing the things we are doing now.

Then, once it is time to move into something else, God will let us know. If we have no new direction, then that is direction. That is really the main point of the entire book.

Who Are You Serving?

One thing that will really help us, is for us to focus on Who we are serving and not to focus so much on what we are doing. Whatever we are doing to serve God and help to advance His Kingdom is good and important.

By keeping our focus in the right place, it will help us to do what we know to do now, as well as prepare us for the future. Again, God is smart enough to know when we need to move forward, so we can trust Him to let us know what we need to know, when we need to know it.

Colossians 3:23-24 (NKJV)
23 And whatever you do, do it heartily, as to the Lord and not to men,
24 knowing that from the Lord you will receive the reward of the inheritance; for you serve the Lord Christ.

We need to do what we do for God; He is our ultimate "boss" and He is the One who directs us in what we should do. No matter who our natural leader, or boss, is, we need to remember that God is the One we are really serving.

Whatever God has us doing right now is valuable to Him and that is how we should look at it. If we will fully commit ourselves to serve God, and others, the best we can where we are now, doing whatever it is we are doing, we will not only be a help to others, but we will be a success in our own life as well.

Stepping Stones Or Building Blocks?

If our view of what we are doing now is that it is just a stepping stone to something else, then we are not fully committing ourselves to serve God the way that we should. That is something I have seen happen several times.

The result is often that whatever someone is doing now is not as good as it could be, and as a result those people are not equipped the way that they should be for what God wants them to do in the future.

And, if we have the wrong mentality about what we are doing, are we really going to do our best or are we just going to do what we have to do so that we can go through the experience to get to something else? People with that kind of mentality never go very far.

Rather than looking at what we are currently doing for God as just a stepping stone, we need to see it as a building block and do what we are doing as if it is exactly what God has planned for us to do for our entire life. We may not do what we are doing now for the rest of our life, but to do things right, we should view our current work as if it was our life's calling.

In the first few years of my Christian life, and even in the church I worked in after Bible school, the main thing I was involved in was working with teenagers. There were some other things that I was involved in, but youth ministry was the main emphasis of my ministry time.

Back then, I really did not understand a lot about how God could lead me in my life, so I figured whatever I was able to do, would be what I would do. I never really started looking very far beyond what I was doing at the time.

Even though now I could not say that I was ever really specifically called to do youth ministry, because I committed myself to what I was doing and I loved the teens I worked with, I had some success. But even though I may not have been specifically called to do it, youth ministry was available for me to do, so I did it, and I had some wonderful experiences during those years, learned a lot, and made some great friends too.

One time, while I worked in my home church after Bible school, I had returned to Rhema in Tulsa to attend a minister's conference. On one of the evenings of the minister's conference, after the regular service was over, there was a get together for all the youth leaders who were in attendance.

While it was nice to talk to some other people doing the same work I was doing, and to hear what everyone was involved in, there was something I noticed that concerned me a little bit. It is the same problem I see with many people today.

The majority of the youth ministers I talked with loved what they were doing and the teens they worked with, just as I did. But I noticed something in the conversations I had with several of these youth leaders. The thing that I noticed was that many of these youth ministers had been asked the question of when they would leave youth ministry and move on to something else, to "real ministry".

While there were a few youth leaders who themselves were looking to make a move, most of these people had no plans to change what they were doing, but the majority of these leaders had been asked that question by someone else. What was going on? The idea was that what someone was doing now was only a stepping stone to something else.

But we should never look at what we are doing now as just a means to an end, and only a necessary step that we are taking because it leads us somewhere else that we really want to go. This goes back to what we were looking at before, preparation time.

More than once, I have seen people who thought they were ready to move on, and they were convinced they had completed a step in God's plan that was only a stepping stone for them. They did not understand that what God had them doing was a necessary building block that God wanted to use in some way for the rest of their life.

Rather than just do what I did with the idea it was only a temporary thing, that I had to do it to get to somewhere else, I put my heart into what I did and had the idea I would probably do the same thing for many years to come. When the time came that God led me away from that church that I worked in after Bible school, it was difficult for me to do, but I knew that God was leading me to do so.

What I was doing actually was a stepping stone for me, even though I never looked at it that way. But here is the important thing, because of how I approached what I was doing, even though I would not say I was the greatest youth worker of all time, I learned some valuable lessons that have benefited me ever since then.

During this time of working in that church, besides working with youth, I had opportunities to put God's Word into practice and follow the leading of the Holy Spirit in my life. I learned more about

God's Word and how to put it into practice, as well as developing in learning to follow the direction of the Holy Spirit. The Word, the Spirit, and opportunities were all working to help me grow and to be prepared for God's future plans for me.

There have been many times I was involved doing something, often something I was not interested in doing, that I can look back at now and see how vitally important it was for me. For example, my natural personality is more reserved than it is outgoing. If I had my way, most of the time I would just keep to myself and not go out of my way at all to talk to people.

Now, it is not that I dislike people or can't hold a conversation with anyone, it is just not one of my more natural skills. So, guess what I have ended up doing over and over again?

When I was in Bible school, I worked at a restaurant and I was eventually promoted to a leadership position where I oversaw some employees and I dealt with people who had customer complaints. In that setting I had to learn how to deal with all kinds of people.

Even before Bible school, I was the assistant manager at a convenience store. While I was there, I had to deal with customers, and even fill out weekly reports and things like that, which I also did at the restaurant. One thing built on another.

Then, after I graduated from Rhema Bible Training College, I returned to my home church to work as the youth minister and associate pastor. I remember when I first started working at the church and I saw some of the teenagers I would be working with. I had this thought, "They are not going to come over here and talk to me, I am going to have to go over there to talk to them".

Guess what skills came into play there? The people skills I had been developing in the convenience store and in the restaurant! While I was working at those two places, I knew that was not where I was going to work for the rest of my life, but I did my job the best I could and I was faithful, and I was even promoted in both places.

Besides that, in the church, and now with my own ministry, there were and are plenty of reports and papers to fill out. Those experiences I had in the convenience store and the restaurant were building blocks for me that I still draw on to this day.

What if God has not told us anything? Then we keep on doing what we know to do, no new direction is direction. There may be more for us to do in the situation we are in now and more for us to learn.

Ready, Set, Go!

Psalm 32:8 (NKJV)
8 I will instruct you and teach you in the way you should go; I will guide you with My eye.

Isaiah 30:21 (NKJV)

21 Your ears shall hear a word behind you, saying, "This is the way, walk in it," Whenever you turn to the right hand or whenever you turn to the left.

These verses in Psalm 32 and Isaiah 30 are both good verses that deal with God leading us in life. In Psalm 32 it talks about God leading us in the way we should go and in Isaiah 30 it talks about hearing a word to tell us which way to go.

As I see it, both of these verses give the idea of someone in motion and not someone just sitting and waiting. In the Bible, we see how God directs us as we go and that is the key, we need to go and do what we know to do.

Ideas and plans can only take you so far, there comes a point when you have to put some actions to your ideas and plans to make them happen. This is the point we are at as this book comes to an end.

So many people are waiting for someone else to do something for them, or for something outside of themselves to happen for them to be able to move forward in what God has planned for them. Too often we find all the reasons we can't do something, instead of taking advantage of what we can do where we are right now.

A key point that I have made throughout this book is the idea that no new direction is direction. If it seems like God is not giving us any new direction, then that is all we need to know.

When it seems as though God is silent when we ask Him what to do, it can very well be that He has already told us all that we need to know and what we need to do. There is no shame in being in one place doing the same thing year, after year, after year.

But it is a sad thing to ignore God's way of doing things as we try to make something happen on our own. And it is a sad thing to see people venture out into some work that they say God called them to do, only to see them struggle and fail.

As it tells us in Psalm 32:8, God will instruct us and teach us *as* we go, so we need to go! God will work with us as we take the step He has given us, and He will continually guide us as we follow His will.

As Isaiah 30:21 says, when we turn to the right or the left, God will show us the way to go, but that means we have to be either going to the right or the left. As we move forward with God, He will always help to keep us on the right track; remember what we saw in Philippians 3:14-15.

God does not tell us, "Create your own plan, do things your way, if you don't like where you are now, just make any change you want". Remember Ephesians 2:10, God has already prepared some things for us to do and it is up to us to do them.

Now, the decision is yours. How are you doing the things you are doing now? Are you doing things with excellence and being faithful in those things? If not, that is a good place to start.

What has God shown you in His Word? Do those things, and continue to spend time reading and studying God's Word.

What has the Holy Spirit already directed you to do? Follow that direction, and be sure that you listen to the leading of the Holy Spirit in what you do each and every day.

What opportunities has God brought to you? Take advantage of those opportunities, and be faithful doing what you are doing now.

If you have ever asked the question, "What do I do now?" I hope that this book has helped you to find some answers. Always remember that when it seems that you have no new direction that there is already some direction that God has given you.

My prayer is that this book has helped you in your quest to find God's plan and to better understand how He leads and guides you. My further desire is that you not only find, but do His will and lead the fulfilling and satisfying life that God had planned for you from the foundation of the world!

Printed in Great Britain
by Amazon